LET'S FIND OUT! OUR DYNAMIC EARTH

THE WATER CYCLE

I0901242

KRISTINA LYN HEITKAMP

Britannica Educational Publishing

IN ASSOCIATION WITH

ROSEN EDUCATIONAL SERVICES

Published in 2018 by Britannica Educational Publishing (a trademark of Encyclopædia Britannica, Inc.) in association with The Rosen Publishing Group, Inc.
29 East 21st Street, New York, NY 10010

Distributed exclusively by Rosen Publishing.
To see additional Britannica Educational Publishing titles, go to rosenpublishing.com.

First Edition

Britannica Educational Publishing
J.E. Luebering: Executive Director, Core Editorial
Mary Rose McCudden: Editor, Britannica Student Encyclopedia

Rosen Publishing
Amelie von Zumbusch: Editor
Nelson Sá: Art Director
Nicole Russo-Duca: Designer & Book Layout
Cindy Reiman: Photography Manager
Sherri Jackson: Photo Researcher

Library of Congress Cataloging-in-Publication Data

Names: Heitkamp, Kristina Lyn, author.
Title: The water cycle / Kristina Lyn Heitkamp.
Description: New York : Britannica Educational Publishing, in Association with Rosen Educational Services, 2018. | Series: Let's find out! Our dynamic earth | Includes bibliographical references and index. | Audience: Grades 1–4.
Identifiers: LCCN 2017016581| ISBN 9781680488395 (library bound : alk. paper) | ISBN 9781680488388 (pbk. : alk. paper) | ISBN 9781538300312 (6 pack : alk. paper)
Subjects: LCSH: Water—Juvenile literature. | Hydrologic cycle—Juvenile literature.
Classification: LCC GB662.3 .H45 2017 | DDC 551.48—dc23
LC record available at https://lccn.loc.gov/2017016581

Manufactured in the United States of America

Photo credits: Cover Merkushev Vasiliy/Shutterstock.com; p. 4 © NASA/JPL; p. 5 Zurijeta/Shutterstock.com; pp. 6, 8, 11, 12, 14 Encyclopedia Britannica Inc.; p. 7 S_Photo/Shutterstpock.com; p. 9 AdstockRF; p. 10 Dashabelozerova/iStock/Thinkstock; p. 13 Antalia/Fotolia; p. 15 © Corbis; p. 16 Pakhnyushchy/Shutterstock.com; p. 17 © iStockphoto.com/Kulkann; p. 18 Sergej Onyshko/Shutterstock.com; p. 19 © iStockphoto.com/Burneingphoto; p. 20 © Pannoneantonio/Fotolia; p. 21 NASA; p. 22 VaLiza/Shutterstock.com; p. 23 © Huimin/Fotolia; p. 24 © Vladislav Gajic/Fotolia; p. 25 © Bronwyn Photo/Fotolia; p. 26 Artush/Shutterstock.com; p. 27 © EyeMark/Fotolia; p. 28 Teresa Short/Moment Open/Getty Images; p. 29 Hero Images/Getty Images; back cover and interior pages background © iStockphoto.com/BalazsKovacs.

Contents

WATER IS ESSENTIAL

Water is the most important liquid on Earth. Nearly three-fourths of Earth's surface is covered with water. All plants and animals need water to live. Water exists in many different forms, such as salt water in oceans and freshwater in rivers or lakes. Other examples include frozen water of glaciers or water found deep in the ground. The amount of water on the planet remains the

From outer space, Earth appears to be mostly blue because of the water that covers most of its surface.

People use water for a wide range of everyday tasks, including washing dishes.

same, but it constantly moves around. The way water moves around Earth is called the water cycle.

People have many uses for water besides drinking. They use it for washing and cooking. They use it to irrigate crops and lawns, to clean streets, and to operate air-conditioning units and heating systems. They also use the power of flowing water to produce electricity.

Compare and Contrast

How are oceans and rivers alike? In what ways are they different?

States and Forms

Water is made of tiny units called molecules, which are combinations of even smaller units called atoms. A molecule of water is made of two hydrogen atoms and

Vocabulary

Atoms are tiny particles. Atoms are the building blocks of all matter.

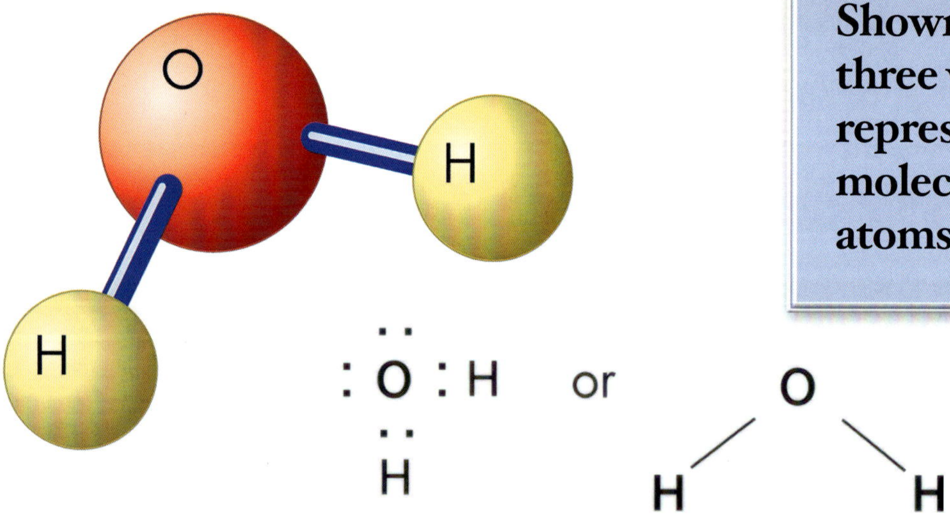

Shown here are three ways to represent a water molecule and the atoms within it.

This glass of ice water contains two physical states of water: liquid and solid.

one oxygen atom. The scientific formula for water is H_2O. Water makes up about 60 percent of an adult's body weight. Water helps the body get rid of waste and maintain its temperature.

Water can be found in three physical states: liquid, solid (ice), or gas (steam or vapor). The molecules in all three states are constantly moving. In snow or ice, the water molecules vibrate but basically stay in place. In rain, the molecules move more quickly but stay near each other. But in steam, the molecules move so quickly that they fly away in all directions.

Boiling and Freezing

Heat changes water from one physical state to another. When ice is heated, the water molecules move faster and farther apart. This melts the ice into liquid water. When liquid water is heated, the molecules speed up even more. Molecules at the surface begin to break loose

Water exists in three states—as a solid (ice), liquid (water), and gas (vapor).

Ice weighs less than liquid water, so it floats on the surface when it forms.

and fly into the air. At most places on Earth, freshwater boils when it reaches 212 °F (100 °C). Once it reaches this temperature, water cannot get any hotter.

Very cold temperatures turn liquid into ice. Freshwater freezes at 32 °F (0 °C). Water is lighter as a solid than as a liquid. This is why ice floats and why it forms on top of a lake instead of at the bottom. Water also expands when it freezes. This is why water pipes can burst on cold nights. The water inside the pipes pushes outward as it turns into ice.

Think About It

Ice sheets called glaciers cover about 30,000 square miles (77,700 square kilometers) of the United States. What would happen if they melted?

Liquid to Vapor

Boiling is not the only way liquid water can become water vapor. At temperatures below boiling, liquid water becomes vapor through a process called evaporation. When the Sun warms the water at the surface of a puddle, the water evaporates into invisible gas. The water seems to disappear, but it actually moves into the air as a gas called water vapor. The main source of water vapor in Earth's atmosphere is the surface water of the planet's oceans.

When a person exhales, their breath has water molecules in the form of vapor. Plants release water

On a sunny day, the water gathered in a puddle will evaporate into the air as an invisible gas.

Compare and Contrast

How is breathing similar to transpiration? How is it different?

vapor into the air, too. Water is drawn through the roots of a plant to its leaves, from where it evaporates. A tree doesn't have a mouth, but instead it has tiny holes in its leaves that release water vapor. This process is called transpiration.

Stomata are the tiny holes on a plant's leaves that release water vapor. They are dark green in this magnified image.

Droplets of Dew

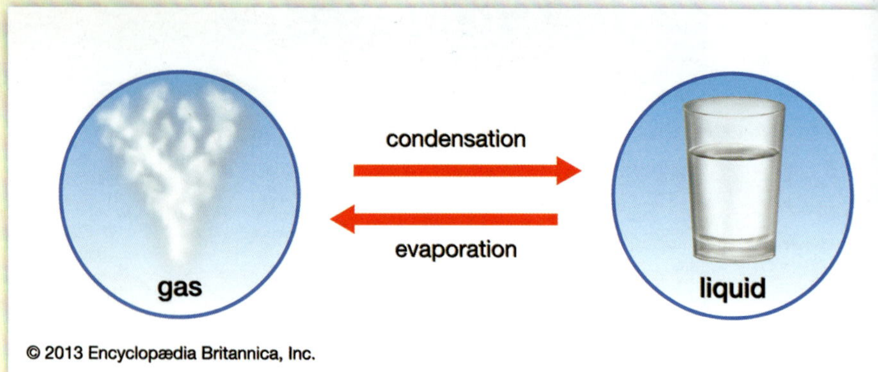

The process by which water vapor becomes a liquid is called condensation. Condensation is the opposite of evaporation. As water molecules in vapor cool down, they lose heat energy and slow down. The slower water molecules collect together to form a liquid. Condensation happens when there is so much water vapor in the air that the air can no longer hold the moisture. Near the ground, water vapor condenses to become fog. Up in the sky, it forms clouds.

In evaporation, water changes from a liquid to a gas. In condensation, water changes from a gas to a liquid.

When warm air passes over cool surfaces, the air cools and water vapor condenses to form dew.

Another example of condensation is the drops of water that form on the outside of a glass of a cold beverage. The drops seem to appear from nowhere, but they actually form from water vapor in the air. The dew that forms on grass overnight is an example of condensation, too. At dawn, tiny drops of water often cling to plants and grass, creating dew.

Think About It

Too much condensation can be harmful. In what ways might too much moisture cause problems for certain places?

The Water Cycle

Water is cycled and recycled endlessly in the water cycle. When liquid water from oceans and seas evaporates, it forms clouds in the sky. The wind pushes these clouds over land, where the water vapor condenses and

becomes rain or snow. The rain or snow falls back to the ground. Water has been cycling since Earth formed.

Though most water is in Earth's oceans, it constantly moves through a process called the water cycle.

Fog is like a cloud, but it is near the ground. It's common in valleys and near bodies of water.

The water in your cup may have been sipped by dinosaurs millions of years ago!

There are three main steps involved in the circular path of the water cycle: evaporation, condensation, and precipitation. Water evaporates into the air from rivers, lakes, plants, and oceans. The evaporated water condenses into dew, frost, fog, and clouds. Precipitation falls to Earth from these clouds. The most common forms of precipitation are rain and snow. Some of the rainwater or melted snow joins rivers and flows down to the ocean or sea, completing the cycle.

VOCABULARY

Frost is a covering of tiny ice crystals on a cold surface.

What Goes Up Must Come Down

Precipitation is the main way water is delivered to Earth. The air high up in the sky is full of invisible water vapor that condenses into clouds. A cloud is made up of millions of tiny water droplets or ice crystals floating together in the air. When water vapor cools, or the air can no longer hold the amount of water vapor it contains, the water returns to a liquid state and falls as precipitation.

Precipitation may come in many forms, including rain, hail, sleet, and snow. The form

Clouds are classified mainly by their appearance. Cumulus clouds are puffy clouds that are often piled up like mountains.

When water droplets become too heavy for the air to hold, gravity pulls them down as rain.

precipitation takes depends on other weather conditions, such as temperature. Precipitation size, speed, and rate are different all over the world. In the deserts of Egypt it may rain less than 1 inch (2.5 centimeters) per year. But in the mountains of India it could rain more than 450 inches (1,143 cm) per year.

Compare and Contrast

How are rain, snow, sleet, and hail similar to each other? How are they different?

Raindrops on Roses

After precipitation falls to Earth, the rain or snow collects in different places, such as seas, oceans, rivers, or lakes. The main sources of lake water include precipitation (rain or snow), rivers and streams, and melting ice and snow. Some water is absorbed by plants and eventually evaporates, while other precipitation seeps into the ground. This water below Earth's surface is

Water frequently flows from smaller bodies into larger ones. Here a stream flows into a lake.

THINK ABOUT IT

Water carves and shapes Earth's surface, wearing away rocks. What examples of this have you seen?

called groundwater. It can reach lakes through openings called springs. Groundwater is a major source of freshwater. By means of wells, humans bring this water to the surface to satisfy their need for water.

Snowcapped mountains also collect water in the form of snow. As the snow or ice melts with warm weather, the water trickles down the mountain and into streams or rivers. The water is warmed by the Sun and enters the atmosphere again through evaporation, and the water cycle continues.

If snow does not melt for years, it may form huge slabs of ice called glaciers.

Water and Climate

The weather found in a certain place over a long period of time is known as climate. Many factors affect climate, including the Sun, oceans, winds, land types, clouds, and human activities. Clouds cool and warm Earth's surface. They work like a blanket and trap the heat on Earth's surface. They also keep Earth cool as sunlight bounces off of them back into space. The ocean also warms or cools Earth's surface. It warms land in winter and cools it in summer because water cools and heats more slowly than land.

The ocean affects the climate of places along the coast, such as Cape Point in South Africa.

These images show a glacier called Muir Glacier in Alaska as it appeared in 1941 (*left*) and in 2004 (*right*). It has shrunk over the decades.

The average surface temperature on Earth is slowly increasing. This trend is known as climate change. It affects the water cycle. Warmer temperatures increase evaporation. This results in drought in some areas and too much precipitation in other areas. In places with warmer winters, precipitation falls as rain and not as snow. Glaciers and ice melt.

VOCABULARY

Climate change is a change in the patterns of weather found over long periods of time on Earth.

The Human Water Cycle

Humans need water for daily tasks such as drinking, washing, and waste removal. The human water cycle explains how people collect, use, and reuse water. Some people get water from a river or well. In cities and towns, water supply systems provide water to residents and businesses. These systems collect, deliver, purify, store, and distribute the water.

Humans need water to live. In fact, water makes up more than half of the weight of the human body.

Think About It

Less than 1 percent of Earth's freshwater is on the planet's surface and available for use. How can people keep from wasting water?

What happens to water after it's flushed down the toilet or rinsed down the drain? It is taken to a wastewater treatment center. There, workers clean it up before delivering it back into the environment and into the water cycle. The workers remove contaminants from the flushed water, such as food scraps, soap chemicals, and human waste. Wastewater treatment centers also clean up storm water from streets.

People do not always have easy access to clean, drinkable water. This is a serious problem in many parts of the world. It is a great effort to keep water clean and available.

Wastewater treatment plants remove chemical or biological waste from water.

Hydroelectric dams harness the swift flow of rivers to create great amounts of electricity.

Another part of the human water cycle is energy. Power plants burn fuels to boil water into steam. The steam powers a machine that produces electricity. Water is also used during the cooling process in power plants. A waterpower plant uses the moving mechanical energy of flowing river water to produce electricity. The up-and-down motion of waves in oceans, or tidal energy, can also be used to create hydroelectricity.

Vocabulary

Hydroelectricity is electricity that has been produced using the power of moving water.

People also use the water cycle for the production of food. Irrigation is what farmers do when they add water to their fields. The water makes their crops grow. Irrigation takes the place of rainfall in dry regions. However, irrigation can also cause problems with the environment. Irrigation water contains more salt than rainwater. Salt can build up in the soil and harm plants. Also, taking too much water to use for irrigation can cause water shortages in other places.

More than half of all farmers worldwide use irrigation to supply the water that their crops need to grow.

Water and People

Deforestation is one way that humans affect the water cycle. When trees are cut down, less water enters the atmosphere through the leaves of trees. In turn, there is less rain. The region may experience drought and other problems. Land with fewer plants growing on it is less able to absorb water. Rainwater washes away quickly instead of being stored in plants and returned slowly to the atmosphere.

Pollution affects the

Forests once covered much of the land shown here in this photo of Madagascar.

Think About It

What can people do to counter the effects of deforestation?

water cycle. People dump garbage and sewage into creeks, rivers, ponds, lakes, and oceans. Factories or cities sometimes release oils, poisonous chemicals, and other wastes into water. Chemicals in fertilizers or pesticides can seep into the ground and make the groundwater unfit to drink. Pollution does not just affect the creatures that live in the water. When people eat fish taken from polluted streams, the pollution passes into their bodies and can cause cancer or other health problems.

Industrial waste that is released into a river pollutes the water. This affects living things and the environment.

Helping the Water Cycle

Water is one of Earth's most important natural resources. As Earth's population grows, water conservation has become necessary. Conservation is the protection of things found in nature. It requires the sensible use of all Earth's natural resources, including water. People need to be careful about how much water they use and be sure not to waste any. Water conservation

Turning off a water faucet saves water. Even a slow drip can waste water over time.

can be as simple as turning off the water faucet while brushing your teeth or taking shorter showers.

Compare and Contrast

How are efforts at water conservation like efforts to keep water clean? In what ways are they different?

People who care about conservation also try to keep the environment clean and healthy, including lakes, streams, and oceans. Planting trees near riverbanks helps to keep water clean. Keeping toxic cleaners and domestic animal waste from water also helps. We can all be responsible stewards of the environment by conserving water and keeping it clean.

Picking up garbage at a riverbank helps to protect the water cycle.

Glossary

atmosphere The layer of gases that surround Earth.

cloud A visible mass of particles of water or ice in the form of fog, mist, or haze usually high in the air.

deforestation The action or process of cutting down forests.

drought A long period of dry weather.

environment All the physical surroundings on Earth, including all living and nonliving things.

fertilizer A substance used to help crops grow.

fog Fine particles of water floating in the atmosphere near the ground.

gas A fluid (such as air) that has no fixed shape and tends to expand without limit.

glacier A large body of ice moving slowly down a slope or valley or spreading outward on a land surface.

hail Small lumps of ice that fall from clouds sometimes during thunderstorms.

irrigate To supply with water by artificial means.

mechanical energy All the energy that an object has because of its motion and its position.

molecule The smallest particle of a substance having all the characteristics of the substance.

natural resources Something found in nature that can be used by people, such as sunlight, plants, or water.

pesticide A substance used to kill pests that would harm crops or that would keep the crops from growing.

pollution Dirtied by waste, chemicals, or other harmful substances.

precipitation Water that falls to Earth as hail, mist, rain, sleet, or snow.

recycle To remake something so it can be used again.

sleet Frozen or mostly frozen raindrops.

steam The invisible vapor into which water is changed when heated to the boiling point.

steward Someone who takes care of people or places.

well A hole made in the ground to reach a natural deposit (as of water, oil, or gas).

For More Information

Books

Hicks, Dwayne. *Finding Water in the Wild* (Wilderness Survival Skills). New York, NY: Rosen Publishing Group, 2016.

McAllan, Kate. *Water Is Precious* (Discovery Education: The Environment Series). New York, NY: The Rosen Publishing Group, 2013.

Olien, Rebecca. *Water Cycle at Work* (Water In Our World). North Mankato, MN: Capstone, 2016.

Paul, Miranda. *Water Is Water: A Book About the Water Cycle*. New York, NY: Macmillan, 2015.

Stewart, Melissa. *National Geographic Readers: Water*. Washington, DC: National Geographic Society, 2014.

Websites

Because of the changing nature of internet links, Rosen Publishing has developed an online list of websites related to the subject of this book. This site is updated regularly. Please use this link to access the list:

http://www.rosenlinks.com/LFO/Watercycle

Index